Bible
Activity Book for Kids

THIS BOOK BELONGS TO:

Christian Faith

thank you!

Dear valued customer,

We hope your child will enjoy our book.

Please consider leaving a review on Amazon.
I would love to hear your feedback as we always trying
to create better and better books.

We read every one of your thoughtful messages, and
reviews are the best way to let other potential customer
know about the book.

We are forever grateful to you!

table of contents:

ADAM AND EVE

Can you find all the words hidden in the puzzle below?

Adam   garden   eat   evil

Eve   serpent   fruit   earth

Eden   tree   good   life

Z	C	A	Z	T	I	U	R	F	F
E	D	E	N	S	L	E	V	I	L
T	T	R	E	E	G	N	E	U	I
C	A	S	M	N	E	A	E	F	V
E	G	A	C	D	T	L	V	L	K
C	D	E	R	W	P	I	E	E	X
A	Y	A	P	K	Q	F	U	J	V
P	G	R	O	J	U	E	B	K	S
D	A	T	J	A	D	O	O	G	A
M	S	H	T	N	E	P	R	E	S

5

Adam is looking for Eve. Can you help him find his wife?

Find the eight differences between these two angels.

they look the same but they are not.
Can you find the eight differences between these two?

Grab some crayons and color Adam by number.

1 - Brown

2 - Light Orange

3 - Red

4 - Green

5 - Light Green

1 - Brown   4 - Blue

2 - Light Orange   5 - Light Blue

3 - Red

Complete the sudoku puzzles.

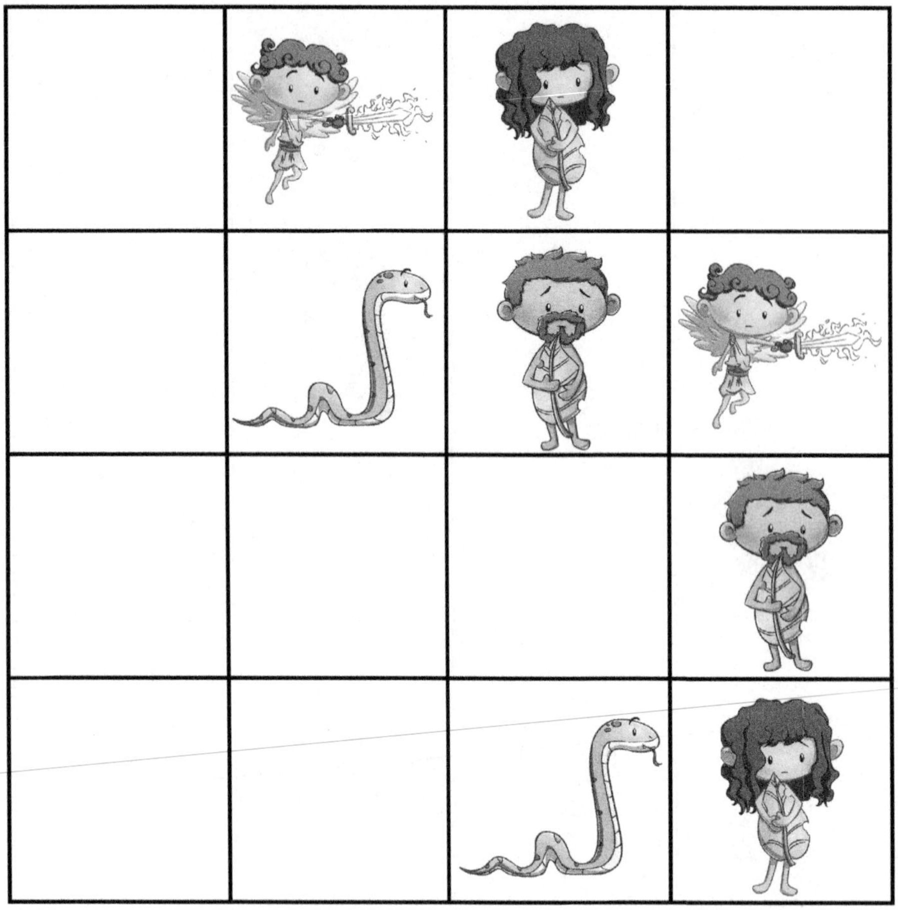

Just color and have fun.

Can you find the right shadow? try to draw a line between the character and the correct shadow.

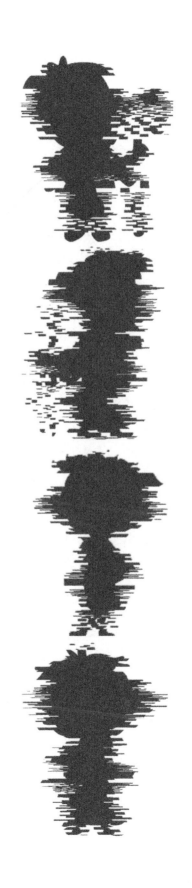

NOAH'S ARK

Can you find all the words
hidden in the puzzle below?

Noah	water	male	dove
flood	Ark	female	food
seed	rain	family	olive

```
D F L O O D N G U N
D O E M R V F O E N
W G O A A A D C A C
O A I F M L H E I H
T N T I Z X E T E I
E D L E E V I L O S
I Y O J R J Z D X A
E L A M E F O X R D
V Q N X M V S K D K
M W T M E R A L F S
```

18

the flood is coming soon and this pair of koala bears
are looking for Noah's ark to save themselves.
Help them find the ark.

Noah sent out a dove to search for land and he found something. Can you help him find his way back to the Ark?

Can you find all the words in the crossword puzzle below?

Circle eight differences between these two pictures.

Connect the dots.

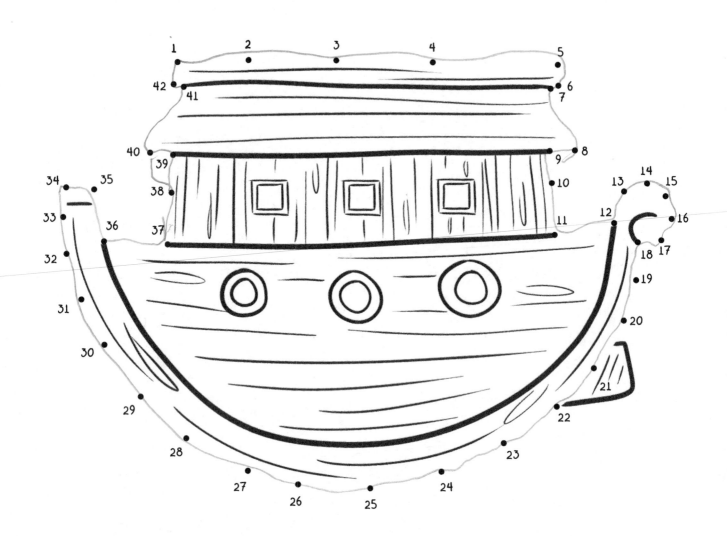

Color by number this rainbow.

1 - Red
2 - Yellow
3 - Green

4 - Blue
5 - Light Gray

Can you complete the sudoku puzzles?

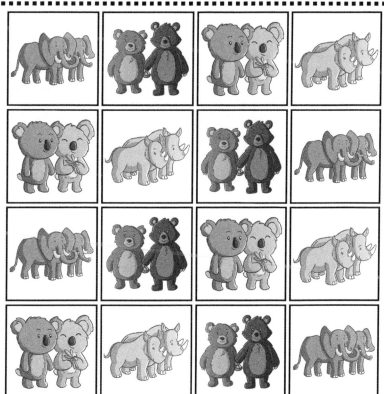

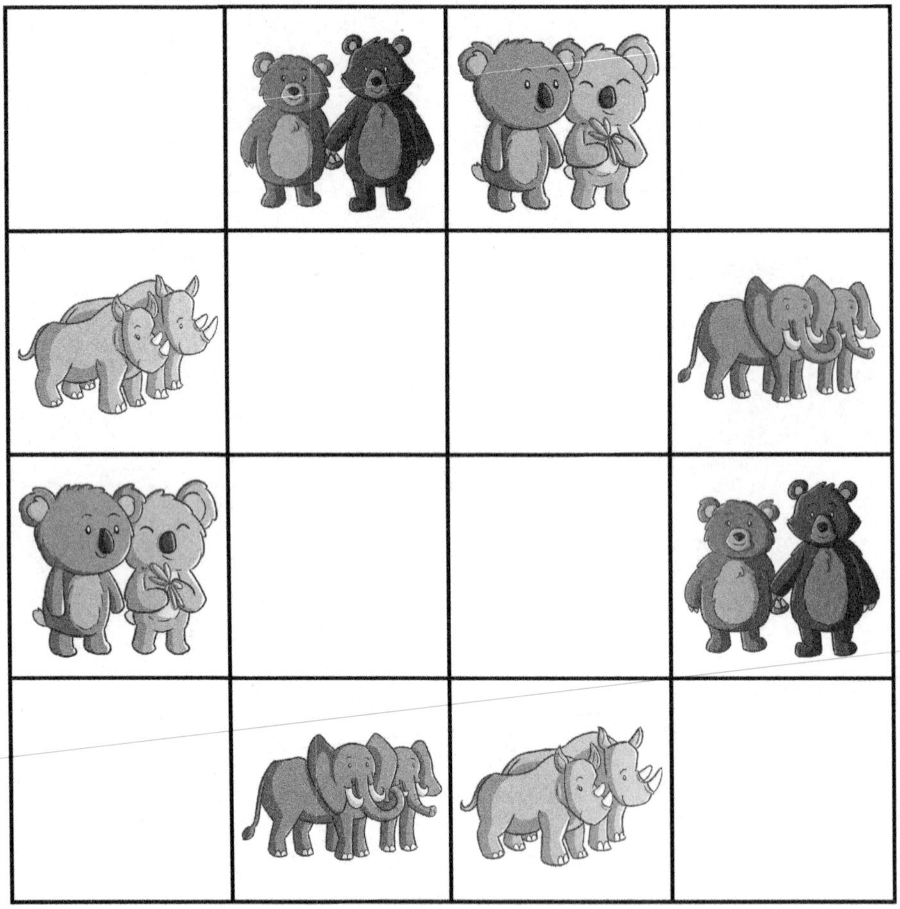

Just color and have fun.

DAVID AND GOLIATH

Can you find all the words hidden in the puzzle below?

David	King	sling	spear
Goliath	battle	armor	helmet
Saul	stones	sword	fight

Z H S T O N E S R Q
D C E Y Y J L O W H
I Q Z L S W M I T S
V E Y M M R H A X P
A L L D A E I O F E
D T S T R L T I G A
Z T A E O O G N Z R
Q A U G V H W R L X
F B L C T Q X S C W
S L I N G K I N G O

this shepherd lost his favorite sheep from his flock.
Help him find his sheep before nightfall.

Connect the dots.

try to find the eight differences
between these two mighty men.

Color King Saul by number.

1 - Yellow

2 - Red

3 - Light Gray

4 - Purple

5 - Light Orange

Can you get this sudoku puzzles right?

Just color and have fun.

Can you find the right shadow? try to draw a line between the character and the correct shadow.

JONAH AND THE WHALE

Can you find all the words hidden in the puzzle below?

Lord	Jonah	tempest	belly
city	sea	captain	pray
ship	sail	whale	land

```
W  H  A  L  E  J  Z  P  V  B
N  H  X  J  T  W  N  J  P  J
H  A  D  C  C  I  X  I  L  T
B  N  F  T  A  L  H  B  I  S
B  O  W  T  B  S  A  Q  D  E
U  J  P  Z  I  P  B  N  X  P
O  A  T  C  R  A  E  D  D  M
C  L  I  A  S  J  L  R  F  E
X  X  Y  O  R  O  L  O  W  T
A  E  S  C  I  T  Y  L  S  L
```

Jonah has a very important message for the great city of Nineveh. Can you help him find his way to the city?

Can you find all the words in the crossword puzzle below?

1.Preaching 2.Praying 3.Whale 4.City
5.Signs 6.Storm 7.Boat 8.Jonah

44

Connect the dots.

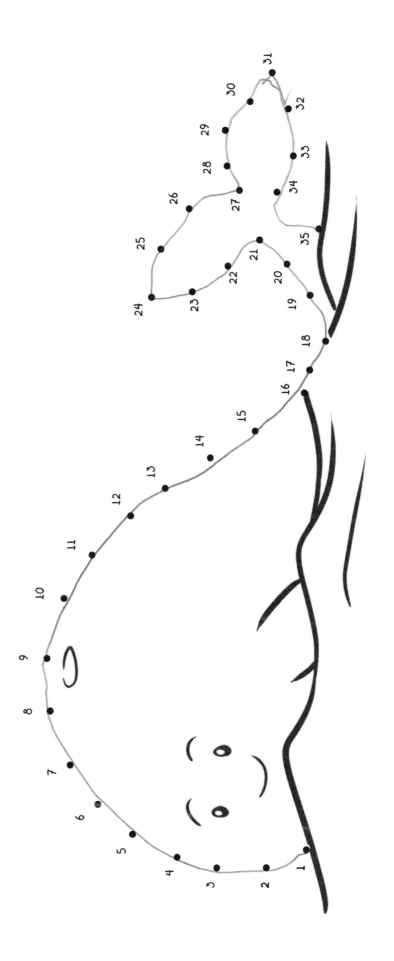

Spot eight differences in these two pictures.

try to get this sudoku puzzles right.

Just color and have fun.

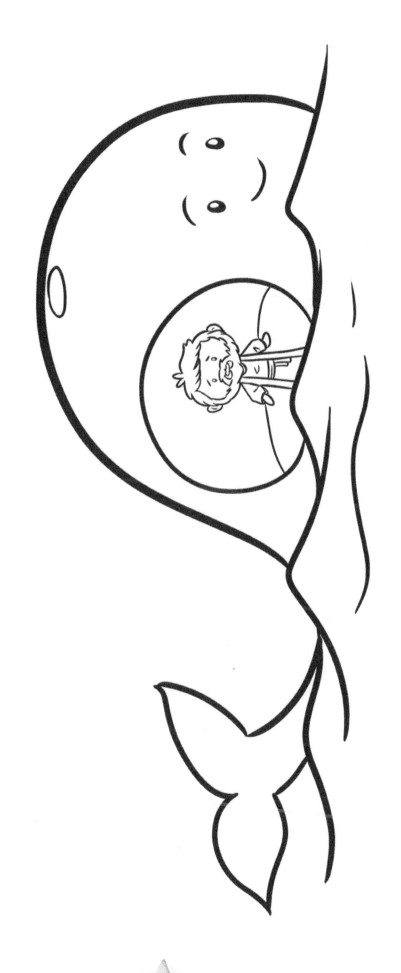

Can you find the right shadow? try to draw a line between the character and the correct shadow.

DANIEL

Can you find all the words hidden in the puzzle below?

lions	Daniel	decree	dream
wise	rescue	stone	praying
order	captain	idol	mystery

R	I	Z	Z	T	O	E	M	A	C
W	E	F	S	Q	E	N	P	Y	A
V	I	S	U	R	D	R	Y	H	P
M	U	S	C	R	G	R	P	I	T
L	C	E	E	U	E	R	R	D	A
L	D	A	V	T	E	S	A	E	I
O	M	N	S	D	I	N	Y	N	N
D	B	Y	R	T	I	O	I	O	O
I	M	O	D	E	I	I	N	T	X
I	N	X	L	O	H	L	G	S	M

Jonah prays to find his way out of the cage.
Help him find the way out before the lion gets to him.

God sends an angel to tame the lions.
Can you help the angel find the way to Daniel?

Spot eight differences.

Connect the dots.

Color the King by number.

1 - Yellow

2 - Red

3 - Blue

4 - Brown

5 - Light Orange

Complete the sudoku puzzles.

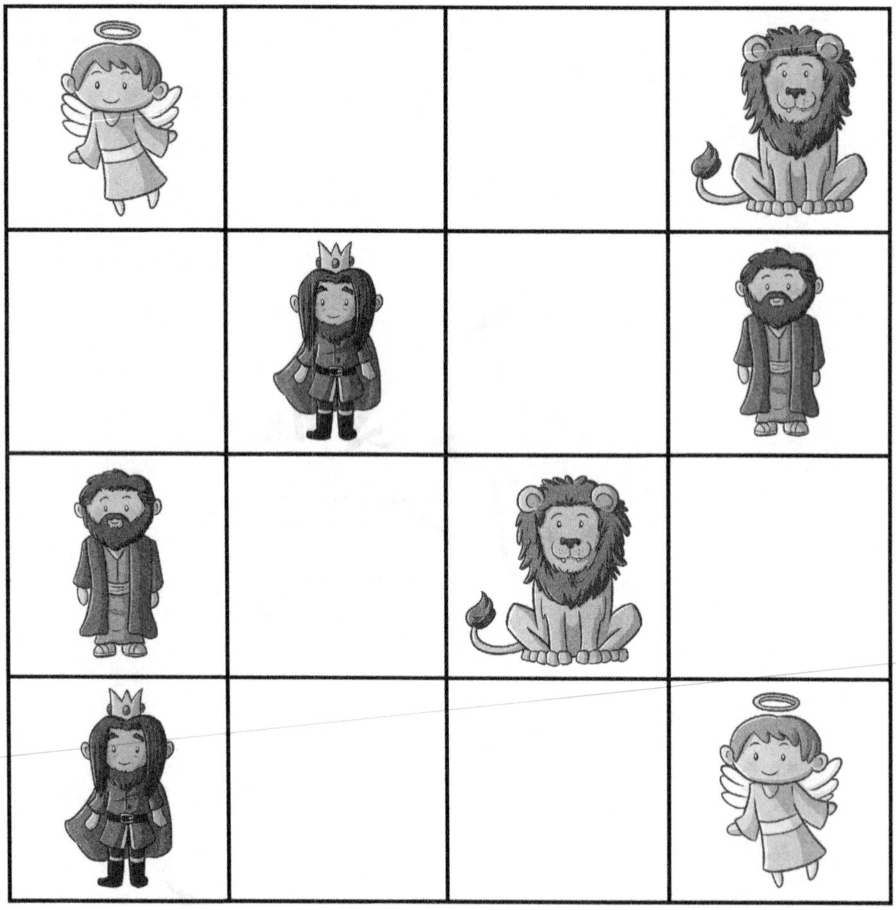

Just color and have fun.

Can you find all the words in the crossword puzzle below?

A SAVIOR IS BORN

Can you find all the words
hidden in the puzzle below?

child   Bethlehem   blessed   greeting
born   worship   babe   kingdom
savior   angel   Son   word

```
Y  N  G  P  I  H  S  R  O  W
I  M  R  A  N  G  E  L  M  S
D  R  E  D  E  S  S  E  L  B
L  S  E  H  J  P  D  Z  K  X
I  O  T  S  E  L  W  I  E  N
H  N  I  A  V  L  N  O  N  U
C  B  N  V  M  G  H  R  R  T
M  A  G  I  D  D  O  T  V  D
T  B  G  O  V  B  C  P  E  N
W  E  M  R  B  L  X  W  V  B
```

Connect the dots.

the three wise men set out to worship the baby Jesus and bring him gifts. Help them avoid danger and reach their destination safely.

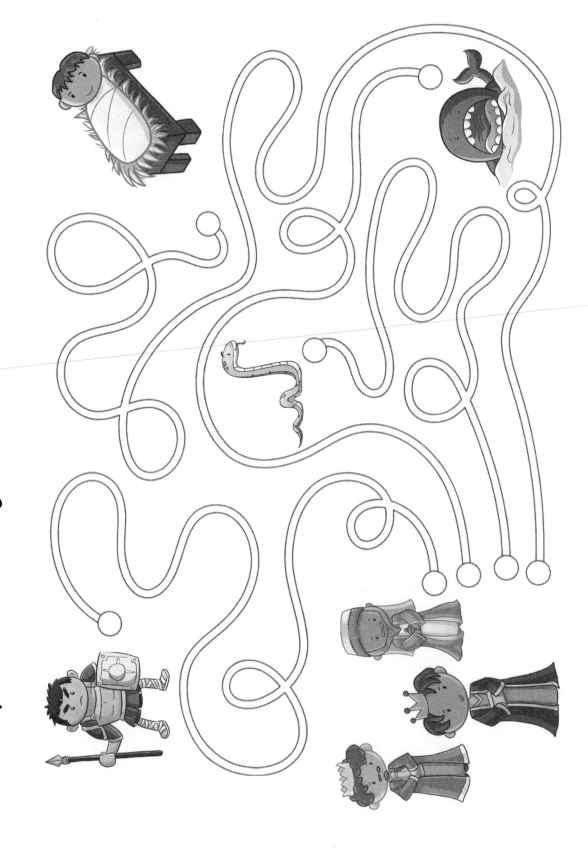

Can you help the three wise men reach the baby Jesus?

try to find all the words in the crossword puzzle below.

1.Angel 2.Joseph 3.Donkey 4.Baby Jesus 5.Manger
6.Sheep 7.Mary 8.Shepherd 9.Star 10.Wise men

Color the wise man by number.

1 - Yellow   4 - Light Orange

2 - Purple   5 - Green

3 - Brown

try to get this sudoku puzzles right.

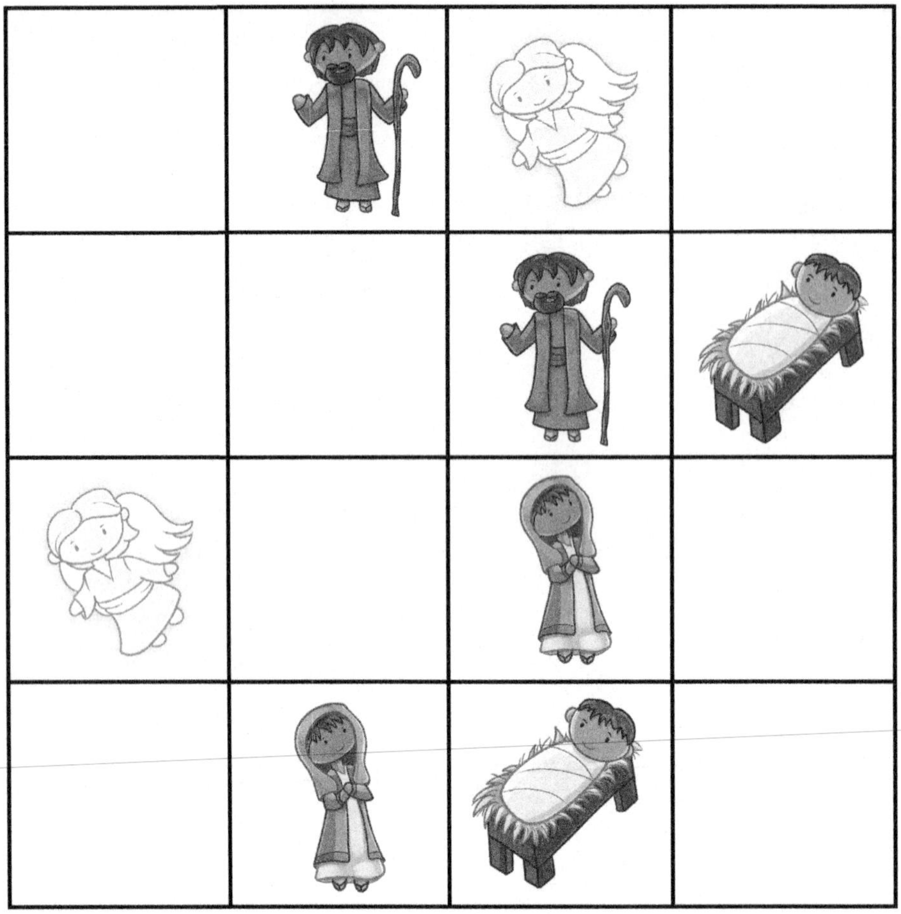

Can you find the right shadow? try to draw a line between the character and the correct shadow.

FIVE THOUSAND FED

Can you find all the words
hidden in the puzzle below?

boat	loaves	baskets	grass
food	fish	evening	fragment
eat	disciples	village	blessed

```
E V E N I N G N D B
Q T A O B C N M E B
F R A G M E N T S A
D P R E P W T P S S
O H L T G Q F G E K
O S O A V A R M L E
F I A E U A L U B T
B F V K S Y Z L T S
E O E S Z A K X I C
D I S C I P L E S V
```

this man is looking for food for his family.
Can you help him find his way to the food baskets?

this kid got lost in the crowd. try to help his mother find the right way to her son.

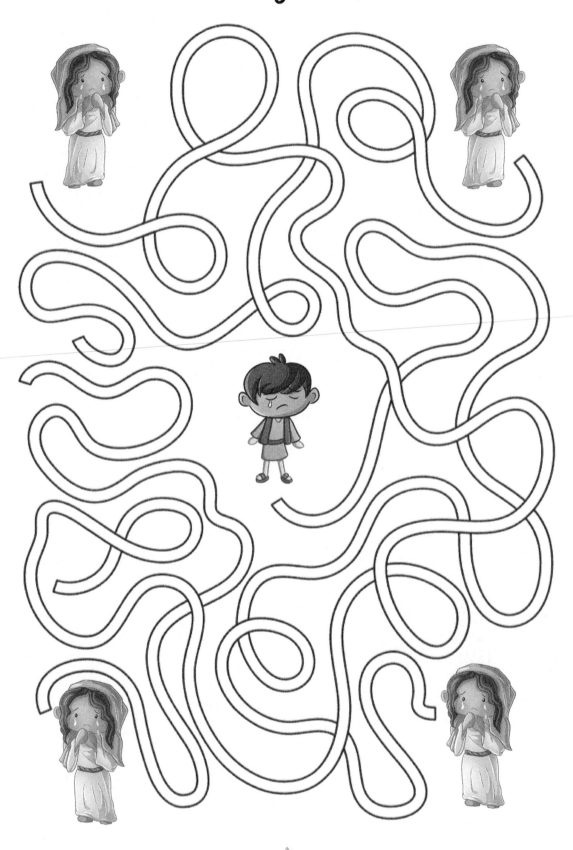

Color this drawing by number.

1 - Yellow

2 - Red

3 - Brown

4 - Light Gray

5 - Light Orange

6 - Light Blue

Can you find eight differences between these two pictures?

Can you find the right shadow? try to draw a line
between the character and the correct shadow.

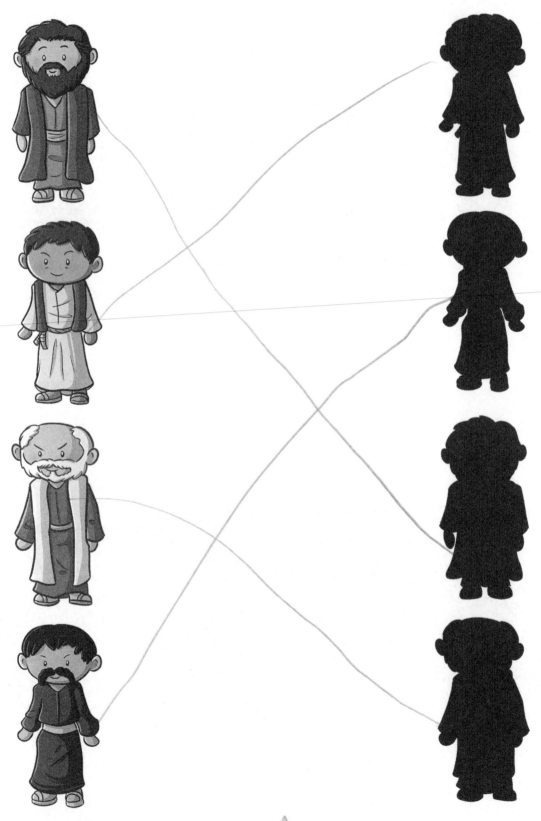

Can you complete the sudoku puzzles?

Just color and have fun.

EASTER

Can you find all the words hidden in the puzzle below?

betrayal   denial   priests   Golgotha

silver   rooster   tunic   crucified

Passover   Pilate   cross   tomb

```
D  P  A  S  S  O  V  E  R  S
R  C  I  N  U  T  G  E  G  T
A  H  T  O  G  L  O  G  C  S
T  F  D  E  N  I  A  L  V  E
D  E  I  F  I  C  U  R  C  I
L  A  Y  A  R  T  E  B  U  R
A  A  L  O  H  B  M  O  T  P
V  A  S  E  T  A  L  I  P  T
B  S  S  I  L  V  E  R  K  D
G  Y  D  R  O  O  S  T  E  R
```

85

Find the path that Lord Jesus took to Jerusalem.

Can you find every child's favorite Easter pie?

Can you find all the words in the crossword puzzle below?

1.Donkey 2.Angel 3.Pilate 4.Tomb 5.Man
6.Woman 7.Mary 8.Jesus 9.Crosses

Find eight differences between these two pictures.

Can you find the right shadow? try to draw a line
between the character and the correct shadow.

try to complete the sudoku puzzles.

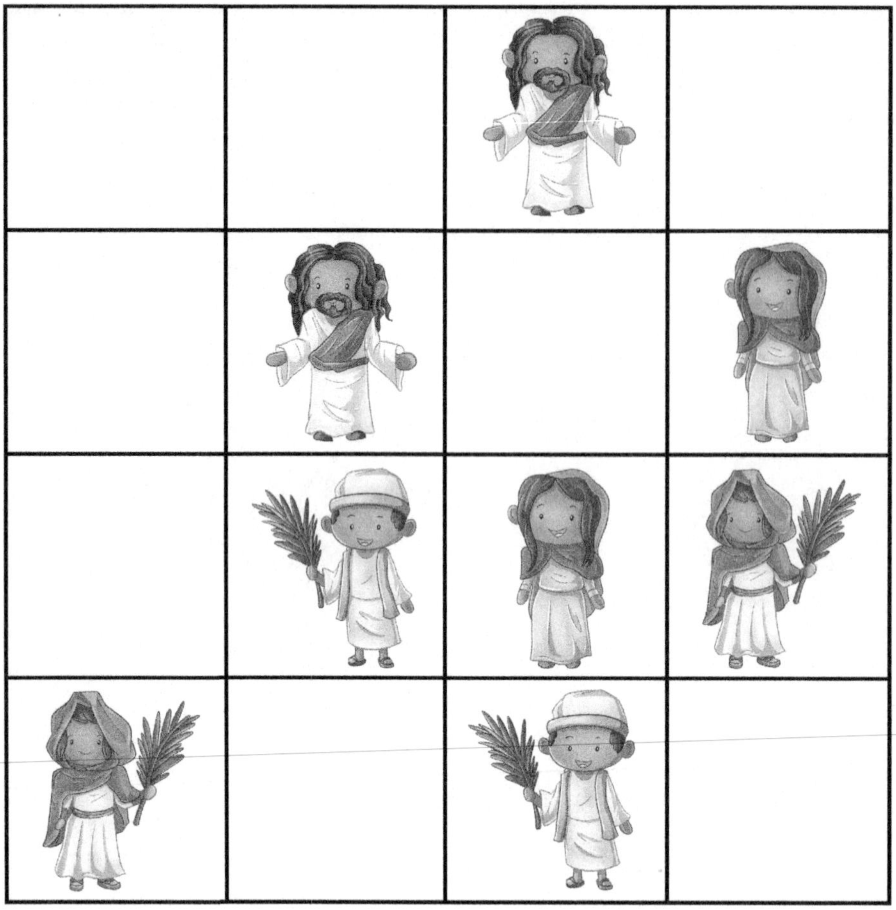

just color and have fun.

Solutions

ADAM AND EVE

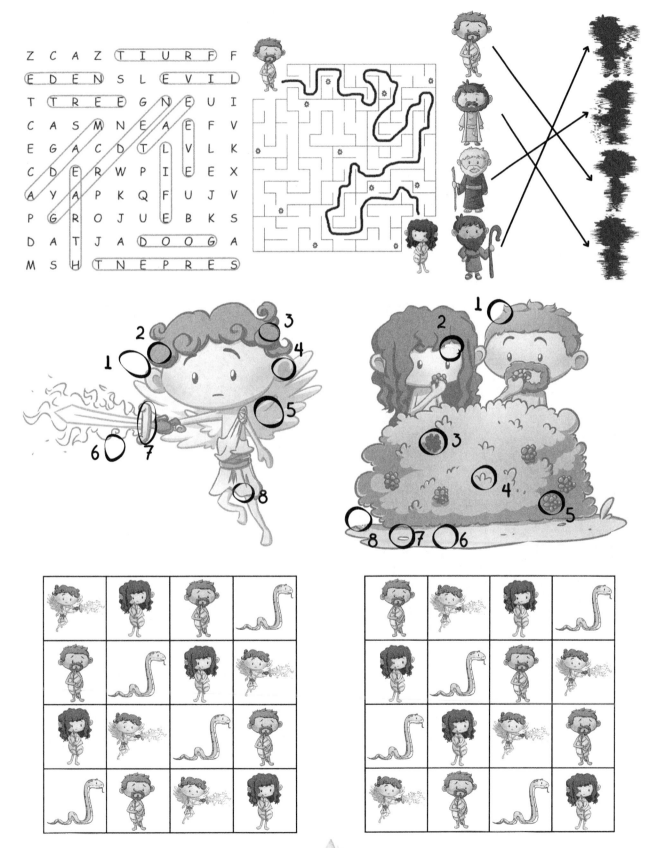

NOAH'S ARK

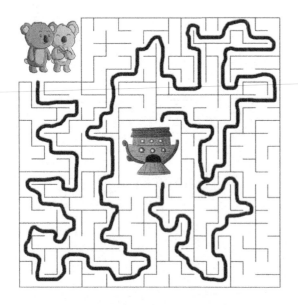

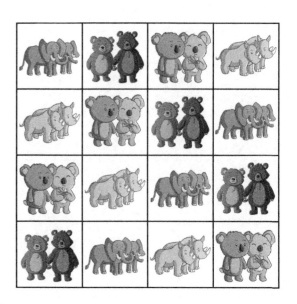

DAVID AND GOLIATH

JONAH AND THE WHALE

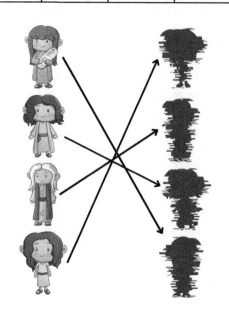

DANIEL

```
R I Z Z T O E M A C
W E F S Q E N P Y A
V I S U R D R Y H P
M U S C R G R P I T
L C E U E R R D A
L D A V T E S A I
O M N S D I N I
D B Y R T I O I N O
I M O D E I I N T X
I N X L O H L G S M
```

1
2
3
4
5
6
7
8

A SAVIOR IS BORN

FIVE THOUSAND FED

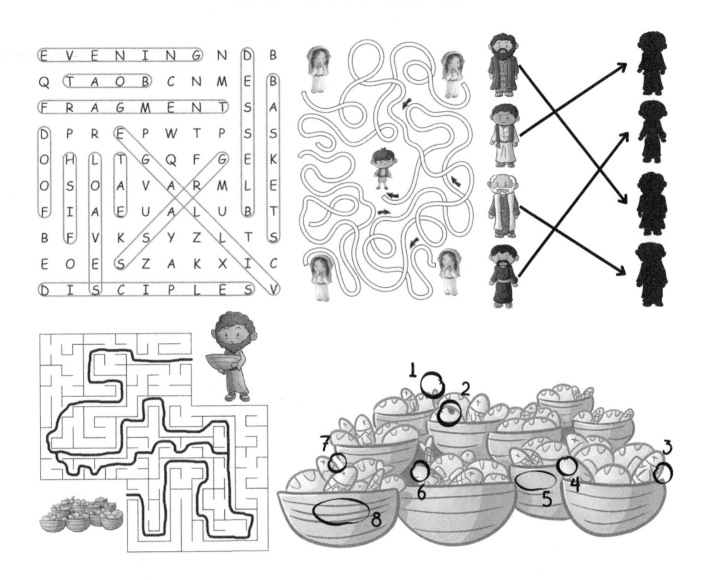

EASTER

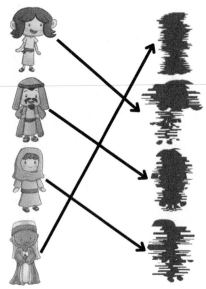

Printed in Great Britain
by Amazon